MW01200452

The Starter Home*

Volume Three

Positioning

The starter home* project began with a question – how could an architecture office, OJT, and and a developer, Charles Rutledge, not only share expertise and in so doing create a streamlined, vertically integrated design-development system, but more broadly, how could we collectively respond to what we perceive as a gap in the market with a spatial logic – one that would rely not only on an innovative view of land markets, regulatory processes, and capital and equity access, but would take a distinctly opportunistic view of the totality of the design-develop process.

As an architecture office, we aspire to participate in the evolution of the typology, to create housing that not only reflects the present moment, but is also simultaneously prescient and aspirational. To design a domestic environment is to have a thesis about domesticity, and we feel that a domestic argument should reflect not only patterns of every-day use, but the ideological, psychological, socio-economic, political constructions implied thereby.

The work in this series of books represents some of the many and myriad inquiries that our office has undertaken as part of our exploration of the "starter home," and our construction of our own starter home* argument. What began as a conversation has been absorbed into the office milieu as a shared, progressively evolving obsession. The following is by no means meant to be comprehensive, but rather implicative of an ongoing investigation.

Positioning, Volume I

The aspiration for the Starter Home* project was for a replicable model albeit not replicable in conventional ways. The struggle we've encountered as the project has grown in New Orleans is the codification of the model as contingent on a specific constraint — nonconforming lots, in this case. Seeing past what is an immediately clear and understandable condition, and into the complex makeup that informs the process, has been challenging.

We are presenting in this volume the critically important expansion of the Starter Home* project to both address the limitations mentioned above as well as highlight what we believe to be a meaningful development of the project.

Editors

Travis Bost
Jonathan Tate

Project Team

Robert Baddour
Travis Bost
Rebecca Fitzgerald
Sabeen Hasan
Lauren Hickman
Marguerite Lloyd
Jessica O'Dell
Charles Rutledge
Jonathan Tate

The Starter Home*, Vol III.

Distributed by OJT:
www.officejt.com

All attempts have been made
to trace and acknowledge the
sources of images and data.
Regarding any omissions or
errors, interested parties are
requested to contact Office
of Jonathan Tate, c/o Starter
Home*, 1336 Magazine
St. Suite 1, New Orleans,
Louisiana 70130.

Unless specifically
referenced all photographs
and graphic work by
Authors.

Portions of this work have
been previously published in
ARPA Journal,
www.arpajournal.net.

James Casabere's "Subdivision with
Spotlight", 1982

Starter Home—Louisville*

Contents

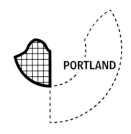

Portland—
Louisville, KY

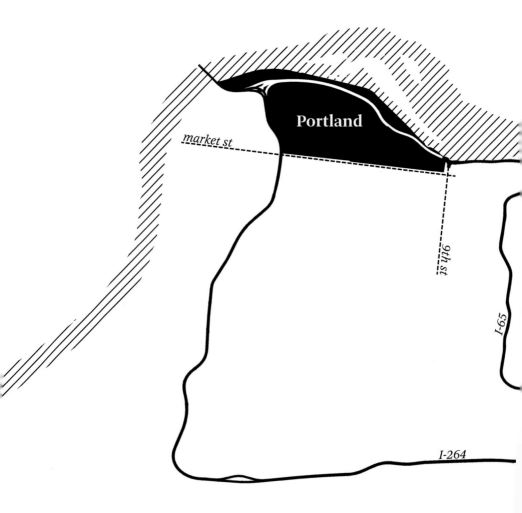

Between Context & Strategy

Portland's fabric drives design & development possibility

Government policy, institutional finance, and architectural convention once aligned to support, albeit highly unevenly, a nearly ubiquitous market system for entry-level housing on a massive scale in suburban landscapes that enabled unprecedented upward mobility. Today, the city—the center of social and economic opportunity—is virtually cut-off to entry-level housing. Louisville* is the latest in a series of architectural investigations our office has undertaken to interrogate this broad conundrum through our immediate and concrete work.

The initial Starter Home* project was launched as an effort to develop creative design responses to entry-level housing types in core urban contexts, sites where—in an unsubsidized market context—all but the highest market segment housing is foreclosed by a variety of policy, finance, and architectural conventions. Much like the mid-twentieth century informational guides of the Federal Housing Administration from which this project is inspired , Starter Home* outlines broadly structured, but formally indeterminate, design frameworks that become the basis of fully realized site-specific architecture. These guidelines are built both out of engagements with and for intervention in the realities of specific urban contexts. Whereas the FHA's Principles for Planning Small Houses, for example, provided outlines for practice in newly opened greenfield conditions of mid-century suburbia, our focus area to date has been the tight urban market contexts of New Orleans' historic core neighborhoods.

---

1 National Housing Agency. *Principles of Planning Small Houses* (Technical Bulletin, Tech. No. 4). (1940). Washington, DC: Federal Housing Administration.

At this stage, the Starter Home* project has successfully developed a number of successful proofs-of-concept in more than a dozen units of infill construction in that city (see Vols. I & II). In this volume, we now turn our focus to a new urban site, Louisville, Kentucky's Portland neighborhood, allowing us to test our loose set of design strategies against a site with an altogether different market and fabric. Our process is an iterative one, developed back-and-forth between research into site and situation, on the one hand, and posited design responses on the other. These five iterations successively produce a 'design thesis'.

Starter Home* is not a prototype—it learns from context.

In giving ourselves this challenge, we have sought to develop the Starter Home as a multifaceted design/development strategy for urban entry-level housing—neither a precious one-off nor mindlessly repeatable type. Our approach therefore never starts with architectural form. Instead research into the problem of housing—not simply urban form—is the basis for our developing a design response. Research does not reveal possible form but possible issues to address in design; the question, not the answer.

Conflicts and limits in the landscape

Whereas the New Orleans Starter Home context typified the high land cost, tight market, and form-restricted historic core neighborhoods of many gentrifying urban districts in North America, Portland's market is antithetical in nearly every way. Three specific challenges emerged out of research which describe a landscape in direct conflict with typical market-driven housing: 'opportunity sites' must be created, not simply revealed; new investments can't retain their value; existing parcels and structures pose competing investment needs. In short, these challenges seem to negate the possibility of any market-based development, much less entry-level market housing.

Overcoming contradictions through design strategy

The response by market-based housing to such 'locked-up' neighborhoods is usually one of three types: abandon the area altogether as an 'unviable market', leaving it to an ad-hoc housing economy; seek out (or demand) public subsidy for housing delivery; or effectively force a change in the market through a large-scale, long-play strategic investment (often with public subsidy) and speculation. Our project eschews these politically and economically dubious strategies to instead work within the context as it exists today.

In response to the seemingly development-antithetical challenges identified, the problem we set for ourselves was to develop design goals and strategies that imagined the possibility for new housing forms in light of these challenges of context. Instead of seeing them as impossible contradictions, we challenged ourselves to think of them as design provocations to be imagined and tested against. Rejecting the typical development strategies that either abandon or rely on uncertain subsidy or imposing intrusion in a neighborhood, we develop design goals that introduce new housing and investment alongside the resident and housing stock that make up the area.

Developing an iterative design thesis

With this set of design goals and strategies we set out to test them iteratively against architectural studies of the site at successively descending scales of Louisville's Portland neighborhood. With each level—the wider metropolitan housing market to a single block and a prospective pro forma—we identify the limitations the context throws up against our design goals while also calling out the empirical opportunities the specific context permits. In the process we develop a 'design thesis' that, as the product of both the broader statement of design goals and the realities empirical context, outlines a way forward for entry-level urban housing in Louisville: "pair on-site uses as leverage to unlock parcels and integrate two markets to build value over time and space."

Design thesis meets site

Finally, this thesis meets the realities of architectural form, the limitation of zoning and form provisions, and the demands of development pro forma in an individual parcel. The iteratively developed design thesis points to a range of possible programmatic arrangements and architectural forms. This phase, currently underway on the ground in Portland will not, however, be detailed here. The articulation of this larger iterative design-research process is our central focus.

Portland— developing a central axis

On the west side of downtown, Portland is a large neighborhood that, while central in location, has historically been the site of deep disinvestment. It has, for this reason, been a haven for unsubsidized affordable housing in the historic core, but it is also increasingly the site of a greater-than-AMI market from elsewhere in the urban core and the inner ring suburbs. Where this district is scattered with vacant lots and structurally compromised or neglected housing stock, these above- and below- AMI markets rub increasingly against one another. A central goal we identified must be to seek out sites and strategies for integrating investment in both these new and established segments. Targeting new infill sites and pairing them with establish and reinvested housing stock, Starter Home here looks beyond any one house to an interlinked system of development that becomes the basis for new housing units and retained investment.

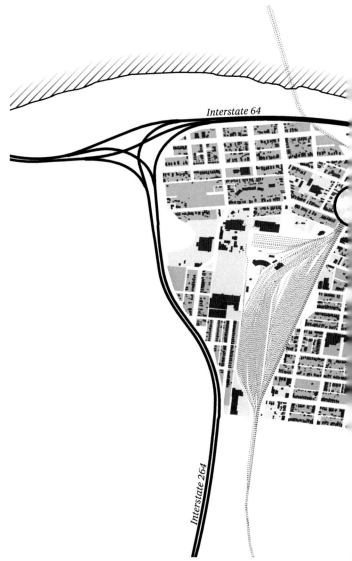

Interstate 64

Interstate 264

O h i o   R i v e r

W Market St.

9th St.

DOWNTOWN

Portland is not an 'opportunity neighborhood'

People live here.

Far from 'open for development' or a 'new frontier', Portland is a long established neigborhood, even as investment has long been withheld. Starter Home* is not entering a 'blank slate' here.

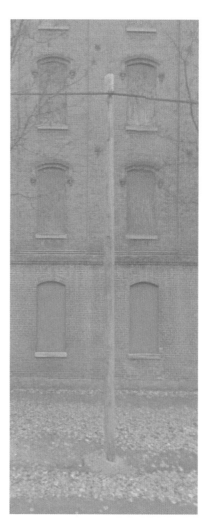

Between active industrial, disinvested residential stock, and vacancy.

1

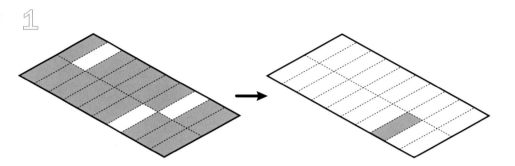

Development Potential is not Hidden, It Has to Be Created.

Whereas in typical core urban neighborhoods smaller or more affordable development sites must be sought out among establised development and larger—more expensive— lots, Portland is dominated by disinvested and vacant parcels.

2

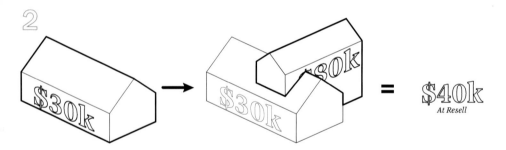

Investment Cannot Be Retained in Future Sale

The broader devalued condition of the neighborhood market works to undermine investment in any one site. Improvements are difficult to justify when their investment value cannot be maintained on site.

3

Competing Investment Needs: Structure Stabilization & New Development

A significant port of the existing housing stock and other structures are in need of near or immediate structural stabilization to remain viable. This reality competes with a simultaneous need for development on the significant number of existing vacant parcels.

Here in quickly shifting Portland, a development strategy cannot be imposed out of the can. Starter development identifies and learns from the challenges of the neighborhood's landscape (above). From the three broad challenges identified for Portland, Starter development draws several design goals:

Make—not locate—potential

Whereas Starter Home*—New Orleans sought out 'hidden potential' in small and difficult parcels in high-demand urban core neighborhoods, Portland abounds with developable parcels. Design must make these sites "make sense" to development.

Hold Value Amidst Investment

Finding and building on a parcel in Portland is the easy part. Historic disinvestment, however, undermines the ability for any new structure to maintain its embodied value and thus forestall infill. Designing for a broader neighborhood investment-retaining infrastructure must be considered.

Build New Amidst—and Stabilize Against—Demolition-by-Neglect

Materially, designing for value retention means designing a strategy for new investment to exist alongside basic needs of the existing landscape like structure stabilization and vacant lot maintenance.

Maintain Diversity Amidst Investment

At the same time that existing fabric is stabilized and supports a platform for new development, that fabric must also be safeguarded against replacement. As these two types of fabric and two separate markets meet in one neighborhood, attention must be paid to balance the influence of the two. Starter development must benefit from typological diversity, not mass development.

Infill without displacement

More than structural diversity, a range of structures and investments maintains a diversity of use, markets, and neighbors. Starter infill must build alongside, not despite, neighbors.

Obstacles in the fabric shape Starter Home* goals.

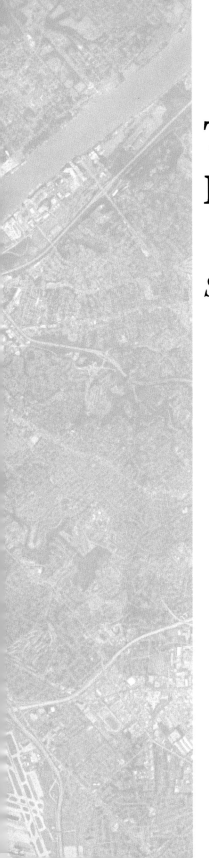

The Louisville Market

Serve two markets.

30-50% AMI

50-120% AMI

Unevenness in value articulates in the city's fabric.

The character of any one core neighborhood necessarily relates to its broader connection with the fabric of Louisville's metropolitan and suburban areas that are both distinct from the city but have influences on the urban core, its fabric and housing markets. Those fabrics are defined by both morphology and market.

The city and suburb both have uneven gradients of value, or "marketability." While they behave similarly, locating the highest marketability to the eastern- and outer-most areas, their internal mechanisms operate independently within each while, at the same time, their markets intersect and shape one another. Despite separate governmental and planning groups, the markets of each drive divergent as well as spillover effects of value and/or disinvestment. Negotiating this interlaced pattern gives form to the design and function of the Starter Home development strategy.

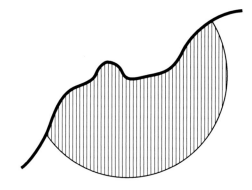

Metro Louisville

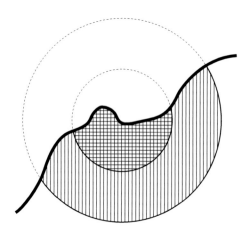

Louisville—City & Suburb

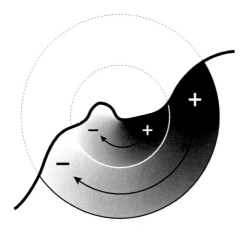

Marketability—East to West

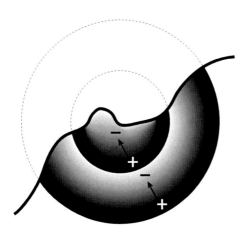

Marketability—Outer to Inner

SOURCE: RKG Associates, "Vacant and Abandoned Property Neighborhood Revitalization Study" (Louisville Metro Government, 2013)

Two areas—and markets—intersect, between disinvested urban core and invested suburban periphery.

These two markets—urban and suburban—do not just operate separately in space and differently in character. They intersect in their unique shape and rhythm, at times synchronizing, at others destabilizing one or the other. More than marketability, the housing stock and market fray along segments of area median income. Uneven supply allows demand to ripple down the chain of AMI segments and classes of housing stock.

An undersupply in the suburbs at the median income level drives this market segment to lower-priced housing that is in oversupply which in turn drives 50-80% AMI buyers into substandard suburban stock or into the urban core where the this and other income levels are already squeezed in the also undersupplied housing stock.

All this leads to a "pushing-in" of mid-level income residents and a "pushing-out" of the lowest income residents in the western urban core. In Portland, two markets have to be considered at once in the housing supply.

Two (intersecting) markets & landscapes

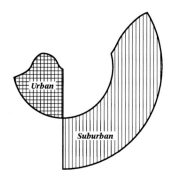

Uneven housing supply by income level and across space

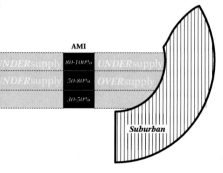

SOURCE: RKG Associates, "Vacant and Abandoned Property Neighborhood Revitalization Study" (Louisville Metro Government, 2013)

*The top of the market is
underserved while the bottom
is squeezed out*

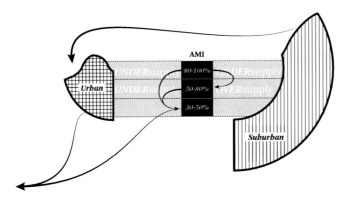

*Uneven housing supply by
income level and across space*

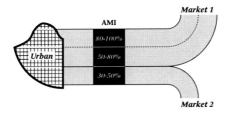

Two markets can exist alongside one another.

Portland District

Engage <u>primary land uses to</u> serve two markets.

residential stock

vacant lot

Segmented markets meet in one neighborhood

Context

As the wider activity of intersecting suburban and urban markets come together intensely in Portland, any development response must take into account this wider metropolitan context at the same time as local concerns.

Here, where metro marketability is at its lowest, an oversupply of land and housing stock meets a "pushed in" middle income market and an increasingly imposed upon lower market segment of residents. These segments meet within an urban fabric that is highly heterogeneous, ranging from active industrial uses to established affordable residential fabric, pocked throughout with a significant set of vacant parcels.

No small district or isolated enclave, Portland is a large morphologically and programmatically varying neighborhood of 773 developable acres (i.e. non-right-of-way). Central to any strategy are the cumulative 67 acres of vacant land that pock the entire district, residential and industrial.

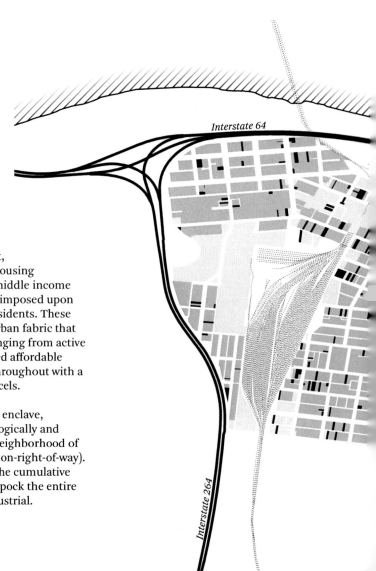

Interstate 64

Interstate 264

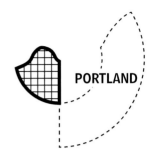

Land Use

■	Vacant
▨	Residential
▤	Other

W Market St.

DOWNTOWN

Segmented markets parallel segmented land use.

Portland—Residential Zoning

Portland—Vacant Parcels

Portland—Infrastructure

Portland Land Composition
Lots by Land Use

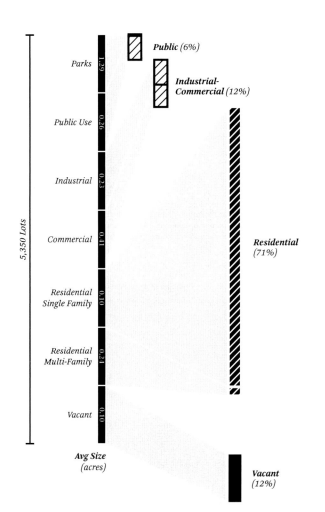

5,350 Lots

Parks — 1.29
Public Use — 0.26
Industrial — 0.23
Commercial — 0.41
Residential Single Family — 0.10
Residential Multi-Family — 1.21
Vacant — 0.10

Avg Size
(acres)

Public *(6%)*

Industrial-Commercial *(12%)*

Residential *(71%)*

Vacant *(12%)*

Where two markets meet, their segmentation is paralleled—even made possible—by many entrenched systems of planning, use, and custom. Cadastral, use, and form designations each carry their own segmenting restrictions on the fabric of housing stock and the shape of housing markets.

A Starter Home that would serve two markets simultaneously must work across these entrenched folds in the landscape, engaging the fundamental categories of urban land. In Portland, the primary components a Starter Home strategy must engage are, of course, residential but also vacant parcels. In total area and ubiquity of presence, these entwined uses are central to the district's landscape.

Vacancy & Variation Dominate Residential Stock

As fundamental categories, however, residential and vacant land uses are far from homogenous or even of an easy typological prescription. The simple categories, 'vacant' and 'residential', fray quickly along qualities of form, occupancy, and especially structural stability. Historic disinvestment has wrought not only scattered vacant lots but also significant neglect of still-extant residential structures, nearly two thirds of which require some structural stabilization. If any refinement is possible, these may be: vacant and stable parcels, and parcels with immediate or near need of stabilization.

The integrity of these seemingly stark categories is further belied, to some extent, by their frequent interlacing in everyday practice. Vacant parcels bleed one into another in great unmanaged swaths, abandoned lands and structures are informally taken over by enterprising neighbors. In the process, any clear of structure of ownership or definition of 'highest and best use' is well blurred on the ground. Starter Home development therefore aims to play off these four articulated categories—vacant; residential, structurally stable; residential, near need of stabilization; residential, immediate need of stabilization—in the formal, legal, and practical entanglements they yield toward the identified goal of serving the area's two intersecting markets at once.

3,653

Residential Lots
By Stabilization Need

STABLE / NEAR / IMMEDIATE

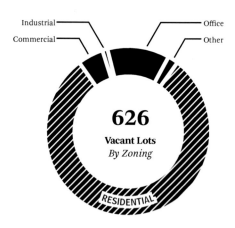

Industrial — Office
Commercial — Other

626

Vacant Lots
By Zoning

RESIDENTIAL

Vacant Lot

New development competes with stabilization.

Immediate Need of Stabilization

Near Need of Stabilization

Stable

Existing Residential Stock

Four fundamental categories of land in Louisville*

Images: Google Streetview

Portland Ave. Row

~~Engage~~ **pair** *primary land uses to* ~~serve~~ ***integrate*** *two markets.*

Segmented markets are planned into the landscape.

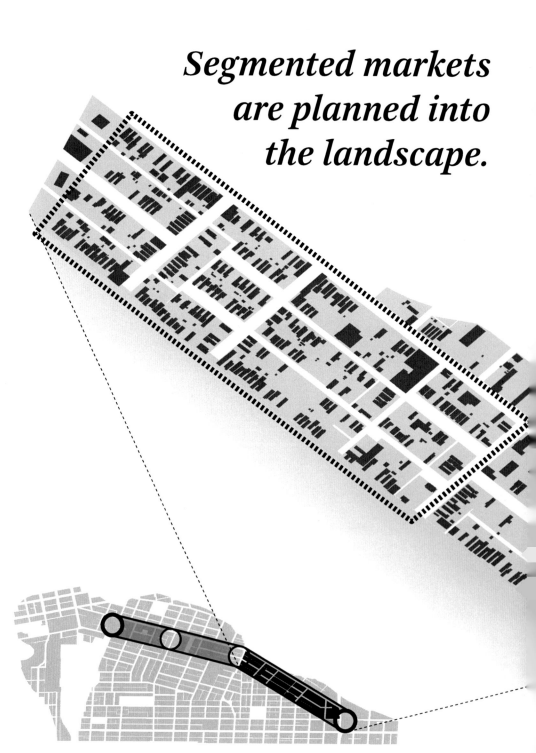

Focusing in on just a first leg of a central axis of development, the landscape remains segmented to a significant degree at every scale from district-wide to that of the block. Across multiple policy areas and indicators, the segmenting effect of each overlays one on top of the other, compounding its effect. And more, as disinvestment has intensified, the hollowing out of the built fabric in all segments has served to still further deepen the segmentation of neighborhood fabric materially, spatially, and economically. Residential blocks shrink over time from their once fully populated height down to a few, scattered still-occupied homes while the simultaneously atrophying commercial and industrial districts relinquish parcels to other or larger uses, withdraw commercial services, and consolidate the few investment-generating activities.

Land Use

Zoning

Form Districts

Vacant

Owner-Occupied

Integrating—not isolating—two markets

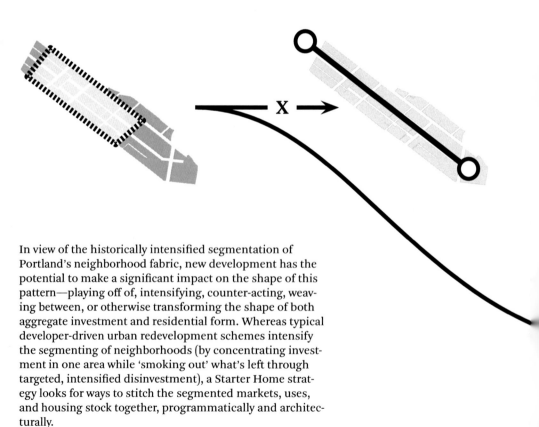

In view of the historically intensified segmentation of Portland's neighborhood fabric, new development has the potential to make a significant impact on the shape of this pattern—playing off of, intensifying, counter-acting, weaving between, or otherwise transforming the shape of both aggregate investment and residential form. Whereas typical developer-driven urban redevelopment schemes intensify the segmenting of neighborhoods (by concentrating investment in one area while 'smoking out' what's left through targeted, intensified disinvestment), a Starter Home strategy looks for ways to stitch the segmented markets, uses, and housing stock together, programmatically and architecturally.

Point-Loaded "Dumbbell"

Typical development strategies in established or previously established core neighborhoods play off of this gap between the more or less 'viable' fabric to target large investments in targeted 'more viable' few sites, anchoring development in one area. This "point-loaded dumbbell" strategy intensifies segmentation in existing fabric by concentrating development at strategic nodes of the corridor—inevitably those zoned to highest use, commercial-industrial—leaving behind the existing market—and its fabric—to deteriorate, eventually to be replaced wholesale by the anticipated new market. This deepens the already-existing "push out" tendency in the neighborhood as part of the state of metropolitan housing provision.

Put Some "Meat-on-Them-Bones"

Alternative to this default strategy, the Starter Home strategy would acknowledge and play off existing segmentation in the neighborhood fabric to spread investment in smaller, more targeted sites, linking the existing fabric. Putting some "meat on the bones" of the existing housing stock over the emaciating default strategy, this tactic would leverage differences of form, parcel, and market to pair development across parcels, markets, uses, or structures allowing for wider dispersal of investment impact, a more stable development, and a more integrated fabric. Ultimately, difference in fabric is leveraged to integrate, rather than divide two markets.

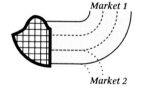

Market 1

Market 2

Starter Home development weaves together segmented fabric to simultaneously weave together housing new and existing markets.*

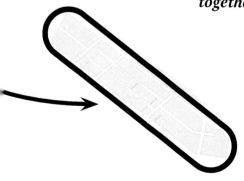

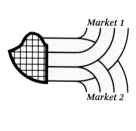

Market 1

Market 2

Portland Ave Corridor

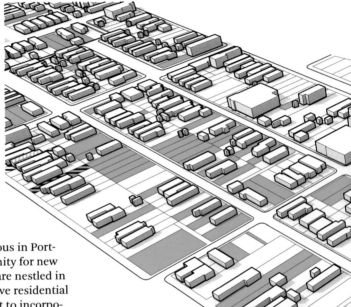

Vacant properties, so ubiquitous in Portland, are an obvious opportunity for new development. However, they are nestled in and scattered among still active residential parcels, making them difficult to incorporate into development in any large or systematic way. At the same time, however, the process for any developer's land acquisition is often equally as scattershot and wide-ranging, driven by the rambling and serendipitous quality in the minutiae of property ownership chains and of the real estate market more generally. Overlaying both these haphazard patterns—vacant parcels, active residential structures, and large land-holding networks—allows us to connect the idiosyncrasies of each in a more coherent, but no less neighborhood-enmeshed, development strategy. This set of tactics allows us to develop a more nuanced, site-specific, and realistic approach to market housing supply, rather than a far more difficult to initiate clearing of entire contiguous blocks for a new greenfield development. Pairing parcel networks, both vacant and existing structures and vacant and developer-held, helps to drive development inertia forward while integrating two markets—the stabilization of existing structures (and affordable markets) and new construction on vacant parcels (a new market).

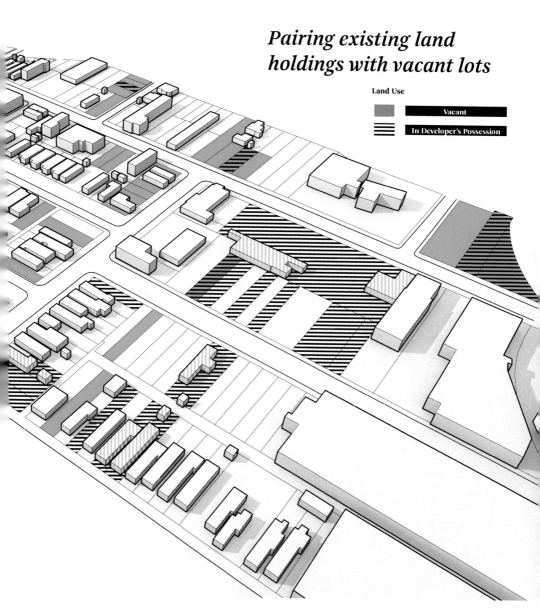

Pairing existing land holdings with vacant lots

Land Use

	Vacant
	In Developer's Possession

Block 015K

*Pair primary land uses to **unlock new parcels and** integrate two markets.*

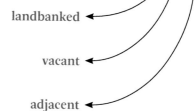

landbanked

vacant

adjacent

In Portland,
Starter Home looks beyond the lot.*

On a block with less than half of its existing parcels occupied by structures, design is, on the one hand, greatly simplified with little to confine it formally or programmatically. On the other hand, any potential investment is subject to uncertainty and potential devaluation originating from the surrounding vacant lots. Any Starter Home response must therefore look, beyond its own boundaries and design intentions, forward to its relationship with these sites over time and space. Anticipating the present and future condition of these surrounding sites ensures that a climate is maintained which aids in retaining the investment of present and any future Starter Home development. The aim is, broadly, a stabilizing of the land—its use and value—in the block. But it is also, more specifically, a strategy that continuously looks forward, anticipating the way development on this initial site may allow new development or acquisition on adjacent lots, building value on the lot as a whole.

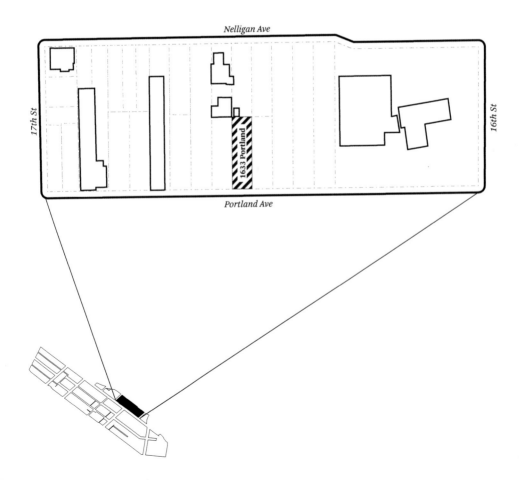

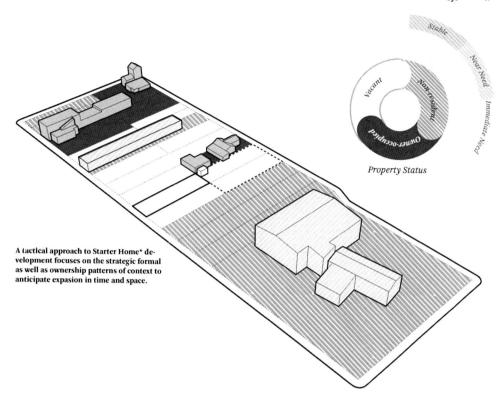

Property Status

A tactical approach to Starter Home* development focuses on the strategic formal
as well as ownership patterns of context to
anticipate expasion in time and space.

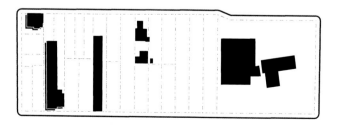

1905 active
units: 50

Louisville, like many midwestern cities,
has been the subject of significant urban
disinvestment. On our block in question
this has meant a net loss of 44 dwelling
units (90%). While this obviously has
devaluing effects on those still active
properties, it also has negative effect
on the block as functional urban fabric,
lacking collective public and commercial
services. As development capital returns,
however, must of the danger is that this
historical loss of density will make for
permanent losses to this fabric through
consolidated parcels, decreased unit
densities, and newly required ancillary
support services (e.g. off-street parking
and increased setbacks). Can this history
be used productively to allow for more
"productive" density?

2016 active
units: 6

Scattered land holdings gain forward movement in development by engagement with a landbank authority.

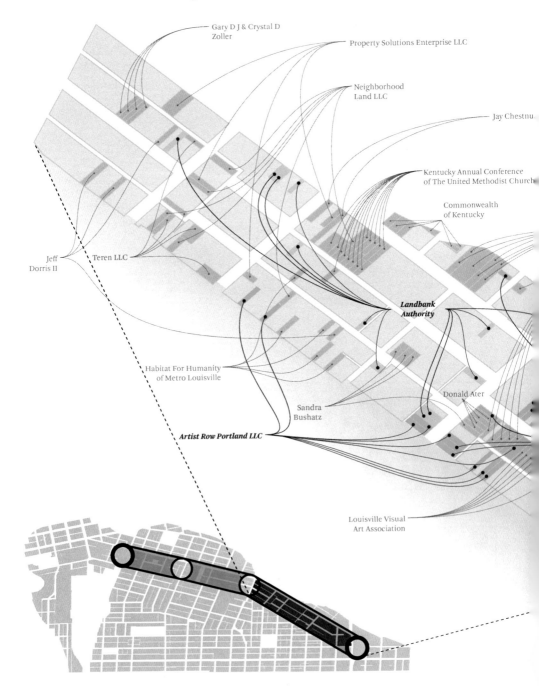

Gary D J & Crystal D Zoller

Property Solutions Enterprise LLC

Neighborhood Land LLC

Jay Chestnu

Kentucky Annual Conference of The United Methodist Church

Commonwealth of Kentucky

Jeff Dorris II

Teren LLC

Landbank Authority

Habitat For Humanity of Metro Louisville

Sandra Bushatz

Donald Ater

Artist Row Portland LLC

Louisville Visual Art Association

Much as it considers the overlapping patterns of ownership and scattered vacant parcels in a wide swath of territory, Starter Home is continuously anticipatory as a design-development strategy. It considers the many patterns of large land ownership, public and private, in the area, seeking out new connected opportunities and adjacencies.

Overlaying this additional pattern of large holdings, makes possible yet more possibilities for expansion in form or connection in program, opening a yet greater range of future development possibility on top of that permitted by considering the pattern of vacant parcels. The weave of these three networks—acquired properties, vacant, and large holdings—introduce greater stability and flexibility into an inherently indeterminate future-unfolding development process.

Starter Home* is an unfolding process, not a single house.

While there are considerable privately-held scattered and/or consolidated land holdings that may be useful for future coordination or investment, certainly the most useful agent with whom to coordinate future development is the local Metro Louisville / Jefferson County landbank authority. The landbank authority serves to aggregate and activate the significant and often difficult-to-assemble/acquire parcels.

As a more flexible tactic, however, Starter Home does not rely upon the landbank alone for potential new sites of expansion, instead layering its opportunity sites along with the scattered range of privately held lots. But not matter the convenient adjacent patterns, neither private owners nor the landbank simply hand over their assembled lots. New sites are opened only by demonstrating momentum in the present-day and potential for the future on the sites currently in hand. Starter Home provides this vision on a given site to incrementally open new ones.

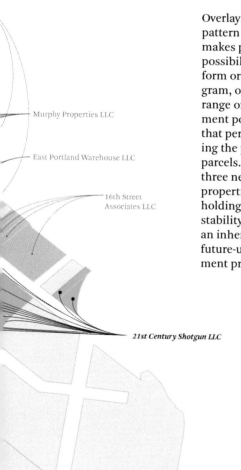

Murphy Properties LLC

East Portland Warehouse LLC

16th Street Associates LLC

21st Century Shotgun LLC

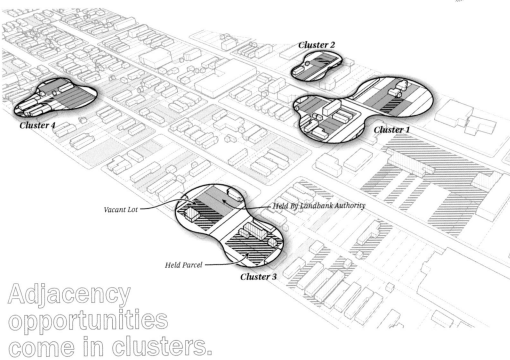

Cluster 2

Cluster 4

Cluster 1

Vacant Lot —

— Held By Landbank Authority

Held Parcel —

Cluster 3

Adjacency opportunities come in clusters.

As the three considered patterns of property in Portland are overlaid, adjacency opportunities emerge in select clusters. These clusters are locations where all three layers align together in close proximity, creating multiple opportunities for expansion and/or programmatic connection.

Adjacency opportunity sites are not defined by an alignment of only two layers (actively held/vacant parcel; landbanked property/actively held; etc.). All three opportunity types must cluster together. In the case of a simple alignment of only two types, if this one possibility does not prove possible, any development possibility of the cluster is denied. The alignment of all three thus allows a flexible multiplicity of possibilities.

Not only does this tactic allow a more resilient strategy overall, it also allows for a multiplicity of type in possible responses, ensuring there is no one generic design response. New development might be paired with a simple repeated design on an adjacent vacant lot while in other cases more complex strategies or designs of adaptive reuse, expansion of an initial project, or an entirely new program or form will be appropriate.

This accommodation of variation within a cluster strategy, in the types of land, program, or form, also has implications for the primary identified development goal in Portland: accommodating two markets at once. This goal may not always be achievable on one initial site. A cluster strategy with more heterogeneous types and adjacencies makes possible multiple strategic opportunities to supply and connect two markets across multiple sites and scales.

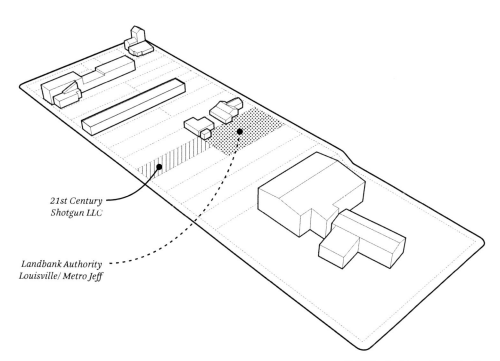

21st Century Shotgun LLC

Landbank Authority Louisville/ Metro Jeff

At 1633 Portland Ave an immediate adjacency is possible with abutting parcels held by the landbank authority.

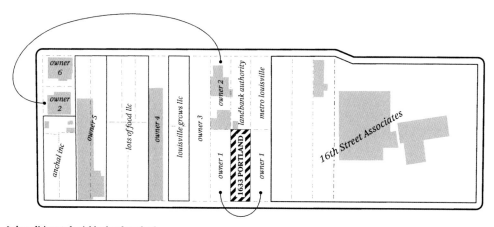

In long disinvested neighborhood Portland, where industrial activity is also present, a great amount of land consolidation has occurred which is both opportunity and limitation to a Starter Home* strategy.

The Market Housing Equation

*Pair ~~primary uses~~ on-site uses **as leverage** to unlock new parcels and integrate two markets **to build value over time and space.***

Redesigning the market housing equation

$$L - C - M = P$$

land cost   construction cost   margin   sale price

Starter Home is not a project of form alone. Setting design-research to the task of tackling the problem posed by the Starter Home project—of urban entry-level market housing—does little if it yields only a model housing type. Setting that same set of design-research focus to its delivery system, specifically the market housing equation, is essential if the types and strategies developed are to see more than a single iteration. The market housing equation here refers to the broad set of broadly economic (but also political) factors whose specific configuration governs the shape of nearly all housing delivery systems in North American, affordable or otherwise. While it has no set, universal configuration it does have a set of few common factors whose relationships can be discussed in broadly generalizable terms.

Understood in nominal terms, the elements of the market housing equation are; Land Cost (L), related to location and the required size of a parcel; Construction Cost (C) in terms of both total square footage to be constructed and the quality of labor and finishes; and Margin (M) construed as the expected rents and returns of equity partners. All this must be balanced against a final Sale Price (P) which—if it is to be considered 'entry-level' in most core urban neighborhoods—cuts beneath the prevailing market of the given area.

Each element connects with the others, though the nature of this connection is never fixed or predetermined, and can be understood as a reconfigurable design element. However, this does not mean that all of these elements are equally or similarly open to design intervention. All are frequently subject to a certain level of "stickiness" in their form, possessing various constraints on their transformation by custom, convention, institution, or other structural factors to the urban market housing delivery system. Whether in the realms of investment, construction, realty, planning, or geography, these constraints are built into the very fabric of housing, making them very difficult to alter. Further, no one element can be changed on its own without forcing cascading effects on the other interconnected elements.

If Starter Home is to be a coherent design strategy it must necessarily open the market housing equation up to design intervention. But, in doing so, it means pushing design hard up against both the entrenched realities of the many extended factors of conventional housing delivery and the complexities of all the intertwined knobs of the market equation's key elements.

Standard 'Affordable' Equation

 — — =

land cost　　　　construction cost　　　　margin　　　　sale price

The standard equation used by unsubsidized developers of 'affordable', or at least below average area market sale price, reduces overall sale price by lowering the quality of finish materials and amenities. Meanwhile, all other factors—at least superficially—remain constant. Land costs remain fixed (usually in line with the standard of the area); overall design is standardized with that of the usual market product so as to always 'appear' comparable while the margin for investors, developers, and soft costs also remains constant (otherwise such a project could not "make sense" in the terms of the market).

While this strategy certain does function in a sense, it has many consequences. These include many that are in fact at cross purposes of the overall goal of homeownership and reduced entry barriers. Cheap housing stock, the exceptional reduction in building material quality, can age very poorly. Materials weather and break, requiring increasing time and money to maintain—at times even outweighing their initial savings—and consequently the investment value of a property is significantly curtailed. Given that, in most cases, assessments for property tax is made by a calculation of square footage of an area average value, a reduction in finish quality will have no long term savings in tax payments.

Nevertheless it is often understandable that this is the default strategy, given that much of the conventional house form is resistant to change. Many of these negative outcomes are often beyond the control of the architect or developer, being instead intrinsic to the market or delivery system itself (e.g. minimum lot sizes, investor expected returns, and realty/cultural expectations of what a 'house' looks like.

Starter Home* controls cost in land and scale— not in finishes.

Starter Home*— New Orleans Equation

 — — =

land cost　　　　construction cost　　　　margin　　　　sale price

The initial Starter Home* project in New Orleans intervened in this standard 'affordable' housing equation in a simple, inverting way. Instead of reducing end sale price at the expense of finish and amenity while leaving intact the basic model (and signifier) of the house, this strategy sought to reduce costs in quantitative, rather than qualitative, terms of nominal land and construction costs. Less land and less built area translate to a reduced sale price, with the consequence that per-ft value increases owing to various fixed hard and soft costs.

All this seems a simple and obvious enough solution to the clear limits of the standard reduction in finishes. However, thanks to the entrenched nature of many of the conventions and restrictions of the housing delivery system already discussed, this is no small feat and a strategy that must be coordinated across the equation elements, rather than simiply turn one knob at a time.

Fundamental to this strategy was a careful knowledge of the historical, legal, policy, and cadastral geographies of New Orleans' urban housing market. In turn, this landscape was negotiated by architectural and policy tactics to adapt a cohesive overall strategy. A rigorous geographic information systems method was developed to locate undersized parcel throughout the city that were subsequently determined to be developable by an existing nonconforming lot clause of the local zoning code, and, finally, an architectural scheme was developed making maximum use of an undersized parcel that was still appropriate to the existing real estate market.

The market housing equation, while a useful outline as discussed above, is in fact revealed to be far more complex when positioned in relation to the scale of time and space in which it operates. Up to now we have discussed the equation only at the most typical scale—a single lot development of an individual detached housing unit for mortgage-backed fee simple ownership and yielding a single annual return to an investor. A much wider array of possible design strategies are revealed when this typical equation is put into context with the must wider range of possibilities revealed in the research into overlapping land use and ownership. The scale of land development and building construction might range from a unit of an existing site to across an entire city while its timeline of development and horizon of financials might range from immediate and no return to a rolling scheme with regular and increasing returns.

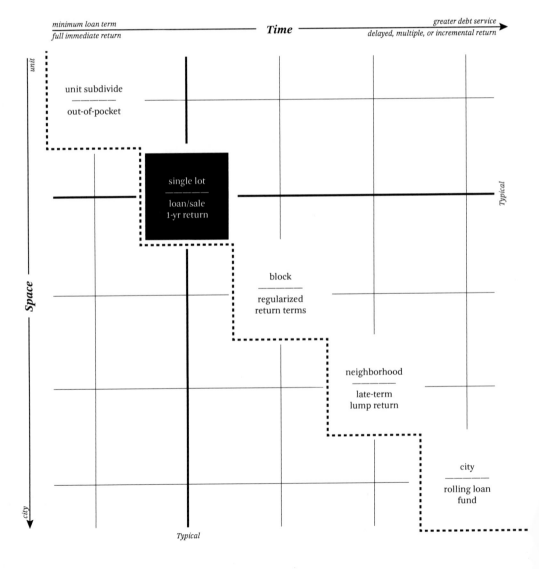

Strategies in Space

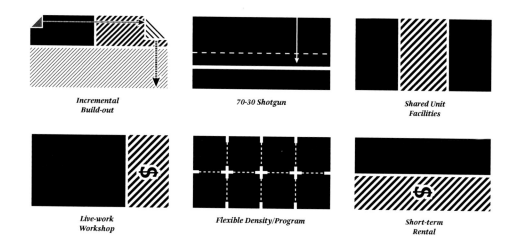

Incremental Build-out

70-30 Shotgun

Shared Unit Facilities

Live-work Workshop

Flexible Density/Program

Short-term Rental

Strategies in Time

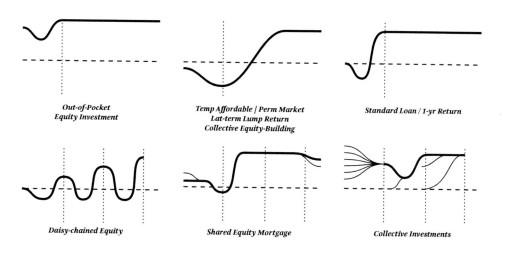

Out-of-Pocket Equity Investment

Temp Affordable | Perm Market Lat-term Lump Return Collective Equity-Building

Standard Loan / 1-yr Return

Daisy-chained Equity

Shared Equity Mortgage

Collective Investments

Scale Of Investment

Socialization Of Return

In Louisville, it is clear that the state of the existing housing market and the specific geography of the Portland neighborhood call for an entirely different consideration of the market housing equation and the scales of space and time at which it must operate. Where New Orleans' core urban housing market was tight and dense to the exclusion of entry-level home price points, Portland, as illustrated in previous sections, is defined by a disinvested landscape that while accommodating both existing and newly incoming markets. Value, overall, needs to be created, secured, and maintained in new and existing construction.

Starter Home*—Louisville redesigns the market housing equation with view to the context that is both extensive and intensive to the site. Low land costs allow development to spread investment across many parcels of Portland, at once stabilizing land costs, debt

Starter Home*— Louisville Equation

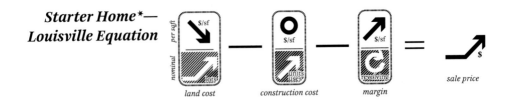

is nevertheless the site of two cross-pur-posed markets. On the one hand, a surfeit of land and structures needs to be stabi-lized against disinvestment, providing for structural stabilization of existing homes and safeguarding of the present sub-market level of affordability. On the other hand, new investments should be integrated into the landscape in a way that retains value service, and fixed investments. At the same time, multiple and varying units and/or pro-gram uses are paired in any one development site to provide for two markets at once, again stabilizing one with the other. Unlike previous iterations of the design thesis, the low cost land here allows Starter Home development to operate on multiple sites at once—simul-taneously or incrementally—rolling costs and returns over multiple cycles, stabilizing the overall development and new neighborhood investments.

Our purpose here has not been to debut a new architectural prototype that might 'save the urban housing market'. Instead, we have elaborated our process for developing a site-situated design-research strategy for thinking the problem we call Starter Home*: developing entry-level market housing for core urban neighborhoods. This chapter has been an important continuation of our earlier work in Volumes I & II on the same question in the New Orleans context. A site that departs greatly from the highly valued, tight market and restrictive historic context found in New Orleans, Louisville's Portland district has challenged this project to test the rule and develop a design strategy resilient enough to encompass the widest range of urban housing contexts.

Here we have demonstrated the process of developing an iterative 'design thesis' which, at this writing, we are now setting to work on a development site in the center of Portland. Here, we deploy a 'loose-type' architectural strategy that is a site-specific response to, on the one hand, the design thesis from the broader state of housing delivery in the Portland neighborhood and Metro Louisville as a whole and, on the other hand, solving the specific idiosyncrasies of the given site. This loose-type strategy is not a tool for developing a single response to this site but an open-ended schema for unfolding investment in a network of architectural forms across multiple sites and cycles of development. In both design process and construction, design research allows us to understand architecture beyond any one site, as a process unfolding in given context in response to a carefully framed research problematic.

Coda

Having developed a framework
for urban entry-level housing
out of mutli-scalar research into
a new context, we now put this
"design thesis" to work at a site
on Portland's main street. This
test continues to unfold on the
ground.

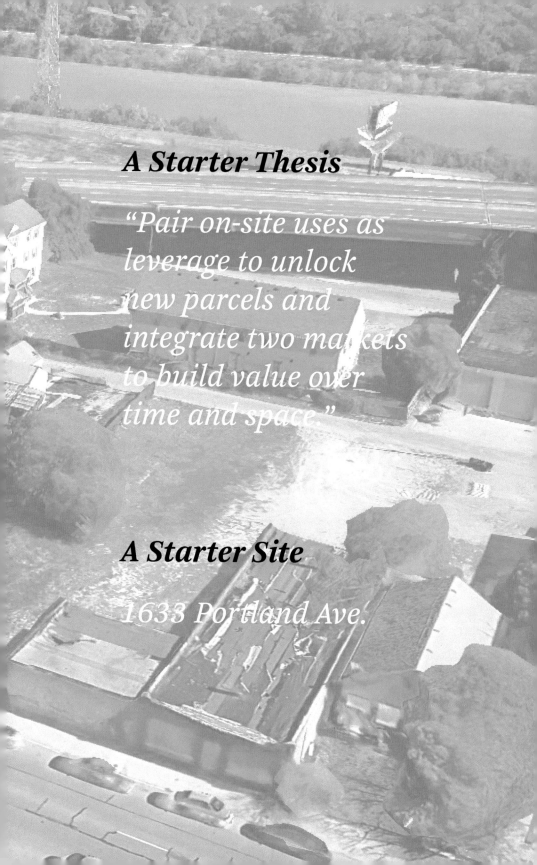

A *Starter* Thesis

"Pair on-site uses as leverage to unlock new parcels and integrate two markets to build value over time and space."

A *Starter* Site

1633 Portland Ave.

1633 Portland Ave.

The contradiction of zoning and infill

In many ways, the central aim of the Starter Home* project, to develop design strategies for entry-level infill housing in core urban neighborhoods, is contradicted by the landscape of Portland's Louisville neighborhood, and particularly in our test site. While, on the one hand, a legacy of industrial use and a recent re-zoning designation permit unusual density for a new infill residential area, but, on the other disinvestment and dimension inhibit the full realization of that opportunity.

The EZ-1 zoning designation permits as many as 16 1-BR units on this site, however on-site parking requirements greatly inhibit realizing even a small percentage of this density despite great underpopulation of area. An expectation of large parcels conflicts with an existing fabric.

Meanwhile, form district guidelines are deceptively optimistic. For much of Portland guidelines permit, as a long established traditional neighborhood, zero minimum

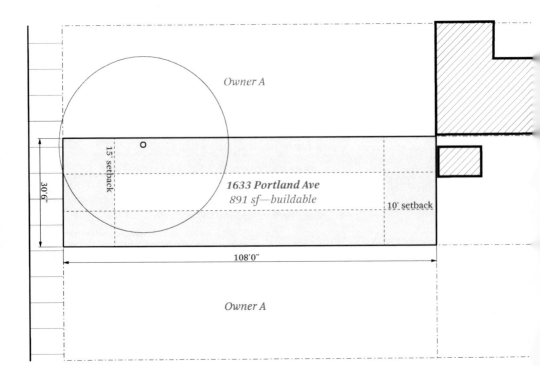

Owner A

15' setback

30'6"

1633 Portland Ave
891 sf—buildable

10' setback

108'0"

Owner A

Historic disinvestment weighs on into a site's future

setbacks for infill development of traditional neighborhoods. However, the impact of long-term disinvestment, abandonment, and demolition has meant that the block on which our site sits no longer meets the definition of an infill neighborhood—one in which 50% of lots in a block face are occupied by principal structures. Of this lot's facing block, only three of the 15 lots have structures—none of which are occupied. In turn, required setbacks, per non-infill form guidelines, are so great as to effectively restrict new development on smaller historic lots altogether. For our lot in question, only 891 square feet of buildable space remain with less than ten feet of developable width.

Finally, shifting ownership patterns—many legacy and/or absentee, many others speculators—constrain any possibility for consolidating holdings in a larger planned development.

With all these factors taken into account, it is clear that a typical design/development strategy is not feasible. Instead a more tactical, anticipatory strategy is needed.

Having, at this point, identified key contradictions of the site and barriers to development, we now refer back to the 'design thesis' developed earlier from broader context research to guide site- and research-driven responses. These 'loose-type strategies' we dub "The 70/30 Shotgun" and "Incremental Infill."

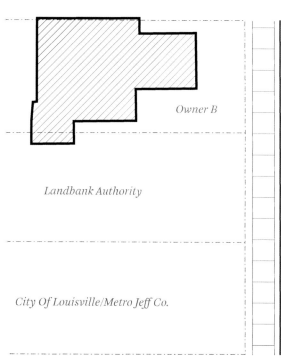

Owner B

Landbank Authority

City Of Louisville/Metro Jeff Co.

Zoning guidelines –minimum lot dimensions & setbacks:

Zoning: Enterprise Zone-1

Min. lot area per dwelling:	200 sf
Max. FAR:	5.0

Form District: Traditional Workplace

Min. lot area:	none
Min. lot width:	50 ft
Max. height:	35 ft
Min. depth of front yard:	15 ft
Min. depth of rear:	15 ft
Min. depth of side yards:	10 ft

Pair on-site uses as leverage to unlock parcels and **integrate two markets** to build value over time and space.

The 70/30 Shotgun

Driven by our "design thesis" developed earlier, and having identified key contradictions in our site for a standard development, the first step is to develop a typological structure on which a more detailed design strategy can unfold.

The 70/30 shotgun is a loose-stype design strategy that immediately addresses the most foundational elements of the goal statement: integrating two markets. Louisville has a handful of standard residential building types, but in Portland the shotgun is pointedly the most prominent. Whereas a standard double shotgun is a mirrored duplex plan of two linear units, here the units are asymmetrically divided to allow a diversity of unit sizes. But difference in size also implicitly correlates with type and use.

The simplistic move of a dimizing wall to one side or another though is only a diagram. A 70/30 shotgun, understood more broadly as a framework for modulating a balance of markets, types, and uses, is a design tool to flexibly support program variety with the ultimate goal of creating a continuously evolving project that is more stable in investment and equitable in access overall. Whereas standard individual lot development of a single or double shotgun functions only to provide spaces for a new—likely full- or above- market—user, this asymmetry aims at keeping a foothold for at least two different resident types.

With this simple, but open-ended, framework established, the project of the Starter Home* design strategy is to think it in as wide a range of possible forms and contexts.

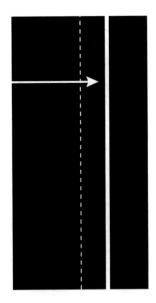

70|30

shotgun

Pair on-site uses as leverage to **unlock parcels** and integrate two markets **to build value over time and space.**

Incremental Infill

Where the 70/30 Shotgun strategy meets one half of the "Starter Thesis" with a loose-type set of architectural strategies acting on space, we approach the second half of that thesis by developing design-investment strategies that work largely across time horizons. Incremental Infill is a context-driven strategy that addresses issues raised through research and formulated through the redesigned 'market housing equation'. First among these is the contradiction of the Portland land market: vacant parcels are ample and affordable; new development is undermined by the depressed values of these and the many blighted structures surrounding.

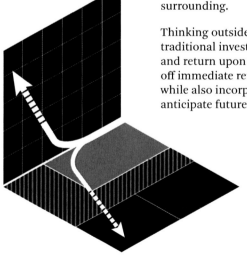

Thinking outside of the standard development formula of a traditional investor- or construction loan-backed financing and return upon sale, Starter Home*—Louisville pushes off immediate return in the sale of developed structures while also incorporating incrementally more parcels that anticipate future accrued value. Incremental infill sets up delayed—not immediate—value across multiple lots in the Portland neighborhood.

Developing a strategy around delayed or even cyclical development horizons interrupts the standard one-year development models and, in the process, opens up a hidden range of strategies related to architectural expansion, capital, and outlay.

Dividing a standard shotgun asymmetrically allows novel pairing of uses or markets within one structure. More than just two standard, yet uneven, residential units, the pairing of these spaces might connect markets or programs that bring greater long-term stability to the Starter Home* development at large or may be leveraged against to acquire neighboring or adjacent parcels for rolling development.

There's more than one way to split a shotgun

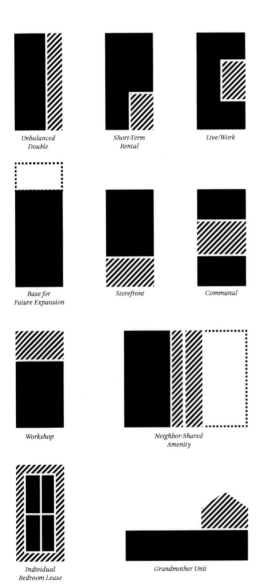

Unbalanced
Double

Short-Term
Rental

Live/Work

Base for
Future Expansion

Storefront

Communal

Workshop

Neighbor-Shared
Amenity

Individual
Bedroom Lease

Grandmother Unit

After a series of iterative and as near-exhaustive as possible design exercises, a range of fundamental qualities emerge for possible formations of the 70/30 Shotgun. Neither prescriptive nor exclusive, any fully resolved strategy will maintain at least a few of these qualities which emerge out of its asymmetric shared-use/type form.

Dual Access

Obviously where multiple units are located together on one site and, more, in one structure, dual access must be provided. However, this provision may be designed for various levels of security and separation as required by type.

Shared Utilities

A key efficiency of a multi-unit shotgun is the potential for the sharing of amenities and utilities while maintaining individual ownership or share. 'Utilities' here may mean any number of elements, from the utilitarian parti walls and plumbing chases to the shared amenities of yards or driveways to the more integrated in shared kitchens, common areas, or work spaces.

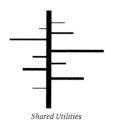

Shared Utilities

Shared Equity

What makes Starter Home*—Louisville substantially different from standard development is the capacity not only to integrate two different unit types and market levels, but also to allow residents of both types to share in the equity of the investment which also has a stabilizing effevt overall.

Shured Equity

Income Generation

Varied unit types may also allow an income-generating use on site, whether live/work or commercial. As a permanent or initial use, this use may generate offsets for affordability.

Adaptability

While the 70/30 framework offers an initial degree of flexibility, a fundamental element of a broader Starter Strategy is to provide for future adaptability on- or off- site.

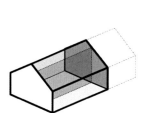

Adaptability

Dual Access

Income Generation

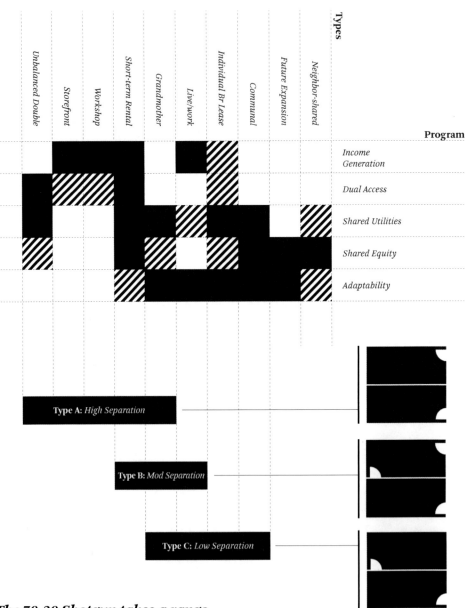

Types

Unbalanced Double · Storefront · Workshop · Short-term Rental · Grandmother · Live/work · Individual Br Lease · Communal · Future Expansion · Neighbor-shared

Program

Income Generation · Dual Access · Shared Utilities · Shared Equity · Adaptability

Type A: *High Separation*

Type B: *Mod Separation*

Type C: *Low Separation*

The 70-30 Shotgun takes a range of types & programs but is defined in architecture by kind & degree of unit separation.

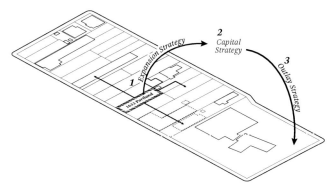

Incremental Infill is a process shaped by context

Opening up the typical one-year development timeline unsettles three interlinked rhythms of design and development that can be re-linked in a variety of ways. These include considering (a) how architecture permits expansion, (b) how capital is amassed whether in bank loans or collective models of shared ownership, and (c) how investment is outlayed, whether in a single site, rolling small outlays, or across a number of related structures.

Expansion Strategy

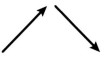
Proof-of-Concept > Repeat

Build Framework > Intensify Use

Partial Structure > Build Out

———— Integration of Land ————→

Capital Strategy

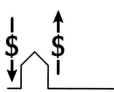
Initial Bulk Raise | Delayed Return

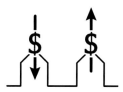
Rolling Raise | Ongoing Returns

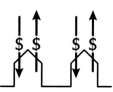
Incremental Raise | Recycled Returns

———— Degree of Liquidity ————→

Outlay Strategy

Invest on Site | Return on Site

Invest on Site | Return Elsewhere

Distribute Investment & Return

———— Socialization of Equity ————→

Site drives type from below;
program drives type from above.

———————————————————————— **High Separation** ————————————————————————

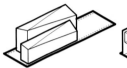

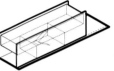

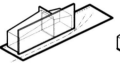

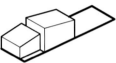

70/30 2-Unit

*Commercial Storefront
(and/or Workshop)*

Workshop

Short-Term Rental

———————————————————————— **Moderate Separation** ————————————————————————

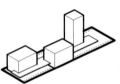

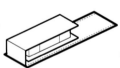

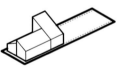

*Commercial Storefront
(and/or Workshop)*

Workshop

Short-Term Rental

3 Degrees of Type

As a loose-type framework—not a prescriptive model unit—the 70/30 Shotgun may take a variety of forms, each the result of an equally varied combinations of site limitation, unit type, program, and market level. Nevertheless, out of an iterative series of possible types and forms, a clear ordering structure emerges which modulates consideration of type. The fundamental ordering factor of this unfolding set of possibilities is degree of separation between units or programs. Each of three designations—High, Moderate, and Low—refers both to, on the one hand, the degree of integration or access between the two asymmetrically divided units and, on the other, the range of feasible unit types and programs. Each designation permits a range of types which overlaps the others to some degree, meaning most unit types or programs may be accommodated by more than one category. A Live/Work type, for example, might be developed from either moderate or low separation configurations. Like the program elements and unit types discussed previously, this categorization is not prescriptive, only suggestive.

Grandma Unit

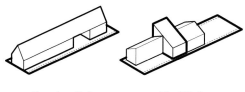

Grandma Unit   *Live/Work*

Low Separation

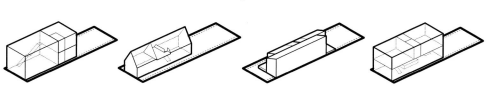

Grandma Unit   *Live/Work*   *Individual BR Lease*   *Communal*

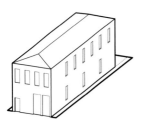

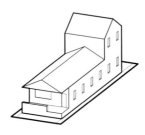

Type A
Flat Box

Type B
Camelback Shotgun

Type C
Standard Shotgun

Local housing types become bases from which starter strategies unfold outward.

Starter Strategies like the 70/30 Shotgun and Incremental Infill are by definition non-prescriptive in form, but instead adapt from architectural types found in the context. Three basic housing types native to Portland are identified above.

Beginning from any of these three types, the 70/30 Shotgun may take a wide range of ultimate architectural forms through its site- and program-specific integrating of two markets or uses in a given site. Type becomes a framework through which the goals of design strategy play out.

Incremental Infill likewise operates as an indeterminate strategy for integrating a new architectural solution into a neighborhood of disinvested properties that can maintain the investment sunk and the existing range of residents.

1633 Portland Avenue is just one possible outcome of the 70/30 Shotgun loose-type design strategy and the context-driven unfolding of Incremental Infill. The specific context and program mix in the unfolding expansion sites may lead to a wide range of architectural forms, activities, and ownership structures.

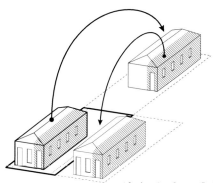

A basic 70/30 Shotgun flexibly allows two different rental market units within one structure. Leveraging against this property releases additional parcels and permits a co-operative, 2-market structure.

Starter Home*— Louisville unfolds over time & space

All at once or progressively over time, multiple parcels are integrated into a housing design that is flexible and interdeterminate in its use, occupation, or future expansion. But while future expansion and new investment in neighboring properties are anticipated in design, that anticipation is embedded into the design of initial structures where multiple uses or unit types are integrated into one structure. These may be of a productive or income-generating type, such as live/work, on-site commercial mixed use, or short-term rental, or simply of a mixed unit type—a traditional market-rate two-bedroom unit connected with an in-law unit, a part-time occupant unit, or a more basic stuio apartment. Together these paired uses both share basic infrastructure of the site, from parti walls to plumbing chases to driveways. Permitting the development to straddle multiple markets at once, commercial or residential, stabilizes the development in space. Meanwhile, the mix of on-site uses supports rolling investment into future structural expansions or new acquisitions of parcels.

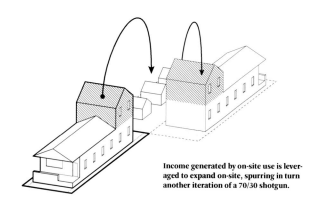

Income generated by on-site use is leveraged to expand on-site, spurring in turn another iteration of a 70/30 shotgun.

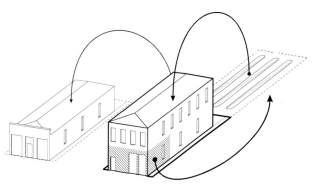

An on-site live-work use is expanded through the acquiring of banked land which drive a stand-alone development.

Loose-type strategies guide concrete connections on the ground.

Our aim here has not been to introduce any one architectural prototype,mathematical and repeatable 'solution' to an undefined problem of 'housing'. Instead, we have sought to develop a framework for addressing the specific problem of entry-level urban infill housing that plays out in highly uneven contexts. Louisville's Portland neighborhood has served as an important contrasting case against previous contexts.

Our extended examination of the Louisville socioeconomic and morphological context yielded a 'design thesis', a clear articulation of what it means to ask these questions in this place. At the opposite level of abstraction, we set about examining the limits to this thesis in a single Portland test site. Between these two levels, we developed neither an over-arching theory nor one-off solution. The "70/30 Shotgun" and "Incremental Infill" are instead 'loose-type strategies' that contingently link abstract development goals and concrete limitations on site.

Starter Home*—Louisville is not a replicable type; it is a loose strategy, built from empirics of site and context research, which unfolds in the specific space and timeline of a given site.

Here at our initial site on Portland Avenue, these Starter Strategies begins to unfold in relation to the limitation and opportunities of the surrounding context. A historical

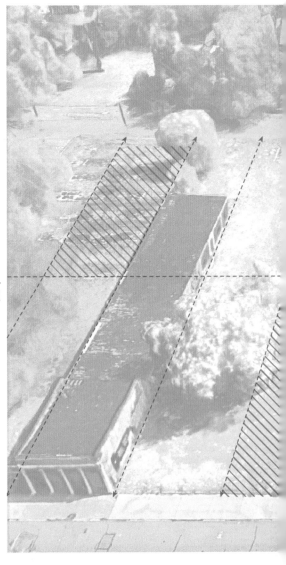

legacy of manufacturing use has meant high disinvestment and widespread abandonment, but also ample cleared parcels and an incentivizing increased density designation. However, the very same force, manufacturing and disinvestment, that makes new opportunities possible cuts at its own roots where abandonment has intensified to the point of disqualifying our test site from infill status and impinges on that potential density. Setting our 'design thesis' to work on this site

and these contradictions yielded a set of design strategies, 70/30 Shotgun and Incremental Infill.

The upshot is a framework for developing design strategies to a phenomenon that spans contexts—tight, gentrified, and historic to disinvested, semi-industrial, and mixed market. In this latest iteration the Starter Home project become a flexible strategy untethered by location.

References &
Works Cited

City of Louisville, Land Development Code (2006 Revision), https://louisvilleky.gov/government/planning-design/land-development-code.

Louisville and Jefferson County Planning Commission, Cornerstone 2020: Comprehensive Plan, (15 June 2000), https://louisvilleky.gov/sites/default/files/planning_design/general/cornerstone_2020_comprehensive_plan.pdf.

Principles of Planning Small Houses (Technical Bulletin, Tech. No. 4). (1940). Washington, DC: Federal Housing Administration.

RKG Associates, "Vacant and Abandoned Property Neighborhood Revitalization Study" (Louisville Metro Government, 2013).

Spatial Data Sources

LOJIC: Louisville and Jefferson County, Kentucky Information Consortium, data.lojic.org.

Louisville Open Data (City of Louisville), data.louisville.gov/.

Develop Louisville, https://louisvilleky.gov/government/develop-louisville.

Louisville Dept. of Public Works and Assets

Louisville Dept. of Codes and Regulations

James Casabere's "Landscape with Houses",
2011

Made in the USA
Middletown, DE
03 June 2023

31724976R00044